Classic Modern Quilts
10 Quilts Inspired By Historical Kansas City Star Blocks

BOOK EDITOR: Jenifer Dick
BOOK DESIGNER: Sarah Mosher
PHOTOGRAPHY: Aaron T. Leimkuehler
ILLUSTRATIONS: Eric Sears
TECHNICAL EDITOR: Nan Doljac
PHOTO EDITOR: Jo Ann Groves

PUBLISHED BY:
Kansas City Star Books
1729 Grand Blvd.
Kansas City, Missouri, USA 64108

First edition, first printing
ISBN: 978-1-61169-109-2
Library of Congress Control Number: 2013950600

Printed in the United States of America by Walsworth Publishing Co., Marceline, MO

To order copies, call StarInfo at (816) 234-4473.

KANSAS CITY STAR
QUILTS
Continuing the Tradition

My Stars
a new tradition

Table of Contents

Foreword

→ By Mary Fons, Chicago, 2013

I consult a dictionary at least 10 times a day.

My job requires that I use words properly, but I keep my dictionary close mostly because I am a word nerd. My word nerd side may even eclipse my quilt geek side. Charged with writing this introduction, I happily ran to the dictionary to look up the word "modern." It was the only way to begin.

Here's what *modern* means: "Of or relating to the present or recent times as opposed to the remote past." Remote past? Why not just "the past"? I looked up *remote* to be safe. *Remote* means "distant past." Ah. So, that which is modern relates to what's going on now-*ish*, as opposed to what was happening in … Elizabethan England? Hmmm.

The trouble with words, glorious as they are, is that they attempt to carve subjective concepts into bite-size *things* that then get whisked into conversation, causing total chaos. Ideas that morph from era to era, country to country, even house to house, get lumped into one word that rarely means the same thing to everybody. Like *modern*, a concept way bigger than the six letters that make it up.

Quilters in the early 1800s made quilts entirely by hand. When the treadle sewing machine came along, those who could afford to get one were considered "modern." Then, the first women with the newfangled *electric* model were the modern ones. The first rotary cutters, the first longarm machines, the first downloadable pattern — all innovations that used to be "modern" and now are just part of the quilter's landscape.

It works the same way with styles. This book is called *Classic Modern Quilts* not because the designers are designing in a specific genre. Some of their work falls squarely into the "modern quilt" aesthetic we've come to recognize in the last 10 years; some of it doesn't. The designs are modern because they exist now, and not in the distant past. (Not yet, anyway.) These are the shapes and the colors quilters are playing with and utilizing today. By this virtue, by their very "now-ness," they are modern.

What is "now-ness" today will be ancient history next week, if the Internet has anything to say about it. In quilting, as in life, it's a good idea to let other people label away while you go along your merry way and make the quilts that please you.

Enjoy this book for the inspiration, traditional, contemporary, modern and otherwise, that the talented contributors have offered with generosity, a quality frequently found in quilters — and one with no expiration date.

＊ ☆ ＊

Mary Fons hails from a prominent quilt mafia family. A professional writer and performer based in Chicago, Mary co-hosts the nationally-airing PBS program "Fons & Porter's Love of Quilting" along with her mom, famed quilter and educator Marianne Fons. She also hosts the weekly online show, Quilty, on QNNtv.com. In 2012, Mary became editor of *Quilty* magazine. Mary believes that being a quilter means being a part of the coolest legacy in American history.

From Tradition to Modern

By now, most of us know that defining modern quilting is difficult, at best. What one thinks is modern, another disagrees with. Then, as soon as a definition can be agreed upon, it changes. That is what makes modern quilting so exciting and fun to be a part of!

At The Kansas City Star, we are known for our quilting tradition. Starting in 1928 and through the mid-1930s, a quilt block was published in The Star and many other newspapers across the Midwest each and every week.

Imagine how wonderful that was for quilters then. Although there were some women's magazines that included quilting patterns, the vast majority of quilting was learned from person to person. Blocks were shared from one quilter to another. Having a new block in the paper each week would have been great inspiration for the motivated quilter.

The original Star blocks ran through the 1960s, but with less regularity by the end. In all, more than 1,000 blocks were published. Then, in 1999, The Star again took up the mantle of publishing not just blocks but patterns for quilts, blocks-of-the-month and other quilt-related projects. The Star, under the Kansas City Star Quilts brand, has published more than 100 quilt books, teaching a new generation of enthusiastic quilters.

Today, just as we always have, Kansas City Star Quilts is keeping up with the times. To serve a significant and growing group of quilters, we have launched a new imprint to cater to the modern quilter looking for a new, fresh creative outlet. Called My Stars: A New Tradition, this new imprint strives to provide the same top-quality quiltmaking books that Kansas City Star Quilts has always produced, starting with this book, *Classic Modern Quilts*.

The Classic Modern Challenge

To kick off this inaugural modern book, 10 top designers in modern quilting were given this challenge: Create a modern quilt inspired by a historical Kansas City Star block. The original block could be changed in any way — to make construction easier or for artistic reasons — as long as at least the connection to the original remained obvious.

With the challenge set, the designers began to create their interpretations of their block based on their personal definition of what modern is. In the end, we received 10 beautiful quilts, ranging from the mostly traditional to very modern. But each is a true representation of its maker and her or his definition of modern quiltmaking.

We hope you enjoy reading about — and making — these beautiful quilts.

☆

Spring Storms

» Designed and pieced by Lisa Calle

» Quilted by Michelle Kitto

» 83 ¾" × 83 ¾"

Based on
Weathervane block
Jan. 9, 1929

In my effort to modernize the Weathervane block, I kept the elements that I like best and that give the block movement. For me, these are the points at the four corners of the block. I added negative space to my designs, so both redesigned blocks are less structured and merge subtly with the background fabric. For the center of the block, I kept the same look of the wreath center, but I set it on point. A simple nine-patch in the second modern Weathervane block design maintains the structure of the block while playing up the negative space. ☆

» Lisa

GATHER

6 fat eighths and 9 fat quarters in a variety of solids and prints for the blocks

5 ⅛ yards of navy blue solid for blocks, background, borders and binding

7 ¾ yards of a dark solid for backing

CUT

Small Blocks

Choose 2 coordinating fabrics and navy for each block and cut the following. Stack the cut units in 4 piles, 1 for each block.

4 — 2 ¾" × 2 ¾" print or solid squares for block center
4 — 3 ⅜" × 3 ⅜" print or solid squares for half-square triangle units
5 — 2 ¾" × 2 ¾" navy squares for block center
4 — 3 ⅜" × 3 ⅜" navy for half-square triangle units

Large Blocks

Choose 3 coordinating fabrics and navy for each block and cut the following. Stack the cut units in 4 piles, 1 for each block.

4 — 4" × 4" print or solid squares (fabric 1) for block center
4 — 4" × 4" print or solid squares (fabric 2) for block center
4 — 4 ⅜" × 4 ⅜" print or solid squares (fabric 3) for half-square triangle units
1 — 4" × 4" navy square for block center
4 — 4 ⅜" × 4 ⅜" navy squares for half-square triangle units

Center Block

Choose 3 coordinating fabrics and navy and cut the following:

1 — 7 ½" × 7 ½" print square (fabric 1) for the center square-in-a-square unit
2 — 6" × 6" print or solid squares (fabric 2). Cut each in half on the diagonal to make 4 triangles for the center square-in-a-square unit.
4 — 4 ½" × 4 ½" print or solid squares (fabric 2)
4 — 4 ⅞" × 4 ⅞" squares for half-square triangle units (fabric 3)
4 — 8 ½" × 10 ½" navy rectangles
4 — 4 ½" × 4 ½" navy squares
4 — 4 ⅞" × 4 ⅞" navy squares for half-square triangle units

Background

From the navy, cut:

4 — 8" × 11 ¾" rectangles
4 — 11 ¾" × 19 ¼" rectangles
4 — 18" × 49 ¼" rectangles

Binding

10 — 2 ½" × width of fabric strips

SEW

Small Blocks

11¼" × 11¼" (finished)
Make 4

Each block is made of 8 half-square-triangle units and 17 squares.

Half-Square Triangle Units

Using the navy and print or solid squares, make 8 half-square triangle units following the directions in Sewing Basics, page 76. Trim to 2¾" × 2¾".

Block Assembly

Lay out the squares and half-square triangle units in 5 columns as shown in the diagram. Sew the columns together, pressing the seams open. Sew the rows together.

Large Blocks

17½" × 17½" (finished)
Make 4

Each block is made of 8 half-square-triangle units and 17 squares.

Half-Square Triangle Units

Using the navy and print or solid squares, make 8 half-square triangle units following the directions in Sewing Basics, page 76. Trim to 4" × 4".

Block Assembly

Lay out the squares and half-square triangle units in 5 columns as shown in the diagram. Sew the columns together, pressing the seams open. Sew the rows together.

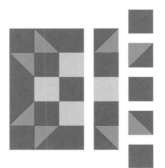

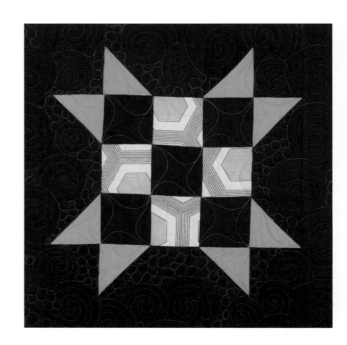

What is **modern quilting?**

⇒ Lisa Calle

For me, modern quilting is an aesthetic and a movement. The types of quilts that modern quilters make are so varied that it is difficult to create a definition that encompasses the whole group. Through my role as the founder of the Dallas Modern Quilt Guild, I've realized that the community aspect of modern quilting is nearly as important as the quilts we make. Because of technology at our fingertips, modern quilters are connected in a way that past generations of quilters were not.

My quilts tend to be a balance of traditional and modern, blending modern fabrics with traditional patterns. I often pair traditional, almost folksy, hand quilting with modern geometric machine quilting. I like to combine opposites in my designs, and I endeavor to recreate the look of thrifted quilts from years gone by when fabric was not readily available in yardage. This means experimenting with imperfectly matched colors, blocks that use different prints when the design calls for just one, and altering the scale and proportions of traditional blocks. I find inspiration in old quilts, online, and very often from my quilting friends, who all have very different styles and preferred techniques. ☆

Center Block

26" × 26" (finished)
Make 1

The center block is made of 8 half-square-triangle units, 1 square-in-a-square unit, 8 squares and 4 rectangles.

Half-Square Triangle Units

Using the navy and print or solid (fabric 3) squares, make 8 half-square triangle units following the directions in Sewing Basics, page 76. Trim to 4½" × 4½".

Square-in-a-Square Unit

Starting with the center square (fabric 1), add 4 small triangles (fabric 2) to each side using the directions in Sewing Basics, page 76. Trim to 10½" × 10½".

Block Assembly

Lay out 2 half square triangle units, 1 navy square and 1 print or solid (fabric 2) square as shown in the block assembly diagram. Sew together as a four-patch unit, pressing seams to the squares. Be sure to place the half-square-triangle units as shown in the diagram so they are in the correct positions to make the star points. Repeat to make 4 identical 8½" × 8½" units.

Lay out the square-in-a-square unit, 4 pieced corner units and the 4 navy rectangles as shown in the diagram. Sew together 3 rows, pressing seams to the navy rectangles. Join the rows to finish the block.

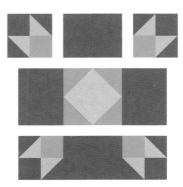

FINISH

—◈—

Quilt Top

The top is assembled in a center medallion with an outer border surrounding it. Refer to the diagram for placement.

Sew the 8" × 11¾" background rectangles to either side of 2 small blocks (Section B). Press to the background. Sew these to either side of the center block. Repeat with the 11¾" × 19¼" background rectangles (Section C). Sew to the top and bottom. Press.

Sew 2 of the large rectangles to either side of the center unit (Section D). Press to the background. Sew 2 large blocks to either side of 1 of the remaining background rectangles. Press to the background. Repeat to make 2. Sew to the top and bottom (Section E). Press.

Backing

Piece the backing fabric into a 97" × 97" square.

Quilting

Spring Storms was quilted with swirls and pebbles to represent hail and a windstorm. Rays of light break through the storm, radiating from the center modern weathervane block.

Binding

Make 356" of navy solid binding and bind.

⁕ ☆ ⁕

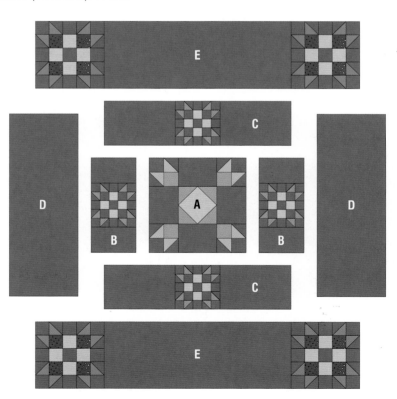

King's Treasure

›› **Designed and made by Lynne Goldsworthy**

›› **60" × 60"**

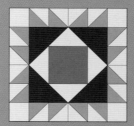

To design this quilt, I drew up the block in a simple black, grey and white design and kept moving the blocks around, adding some, taking some away, adding in other design elements or blocks until I came up with a design which I liked. I chose to use the Shelburne Falls fabric line by Denyse Schmidt combined with Essex Linen in a cream color. The simple blocks against a solid background give the quilt a fresh modern feel whilst maintaining the block's traditional roots. ☆

›› Lynne

GATHER

————◇————

This is a very scrappy quilt, using 3 different prints for each of the 9 blocks. If you want a more controlled quilt, use less variety or mix in a coordinating solid for contrast.

27 fat eighths of different prints for blocks

3 yards of cream solid for blocks, sashing and borders

4 yards of dark print for backing

½ yard of dark print for binding

CUT

————◇————

Blocks

Choose 3 prints for each block and cut the following. Stack the cut units in 9 piles, 1 for each block.

1 — 6⅛" × 6⅛" print square for the square-in-a-square unit

2 — 4⅞" × 4⅞" print squares. Cut each in half on the diagonal to make 4 triangles for the square-in-a-square unit.

8 — 2⅞" × 2⅞" print squares for the half-square triangle units

8 — 2⅞" × 2⅞" cream solid squares for the half-square triangle units

4 — 2½" × 2½" cream squares for the block corners

Sashing

40 — 3⅜" × 3⅜" print squares

48 — 4½" × 4½" cream squares

80 — 2⅞" cream squares. Cut each in half on the diagonal to make 160 triangles.

Borders

6 — 4½" × the width of fabric cream strips

Binding

7 — 2½" × the width of fabric dark print strips

SEW

9 Blocks

12" × 12" (finished)

Each block is made of 1 square-in-a-square unit, 16 half-square triangle units and 4 corner squares.

Square-in-a-Square Unit

Make 1

Starting with the center square, add 4 print triangles to each side using the directions in Sewing Basics, page 76. Trim to 8½" × 8½".

Pieced Half-Square Triangle Units

Make 16

Using the 8 print squares and 8 cream solid squares, make 16 half-square triangle units following the directions in Sewing Basics, page 76. Trim to 2½" × 2½".

Sew 4 half-square triangle units in a row as shown in the diagram, making sure the units are placed in the correct direction. Press seams open. Make 2.

Repeat with the remaining 8 half-square triangle units. To both ends of these pieced units, sew the 4 corner squares as shown in the diagram. Press to the corner squares. Make 2.

Block Assembly

Sew the two shorter pieced units to each side of the square-in-a-square unit. Make sure the points are facing the correct direction as shown in the diagram. Press.

To finish the block, sew the remaining pieced units to the top and bottom, making sure the points are facing the correct direction as shown in the diagram. Press.

Sashing

Square-in-a-Square Units

Make 40

Using the 40 print squares and 160 cream triangles, make 40 — 4½" × 4½" square-in-a-square units following the directions in Sewing Basics, page 76.

Short Sashing Strips

Make 12

Sew 2 cream squares to either side of 1 square-in-a-square unit as shown in the diagram. Press to the cream squares.

Long Sashing Strips

Make 4

Using 7 square-in-a-square units and 6 cream squares, sew together in a row starting with the pieced unit and alternating with a cream square as shown in the diagram. Press to the cream squares.

What is modern quilting?

>> Lynne Goldsworthy

The modern quilting community is a dynamic, exciting place to be. Quilters worldwide connect through blogs, Flickr, Facebook, Twitter, Instagram and other online forums. New ideas can sweep across the Internet and around the world in a matter of days. Online quilting bees, swaps and quiltalongs enable quilters to share ideas and inspiration whilst encouraging each others' progress and ideas. This is what modern quilting means to me — it means quilting today.

Because of the constant fluidity of ideas and trends, any attempt to define modern quilting quickly becomes outdated and irrelevant. So what is modern quilting? Modern quilters value and learn from traditional quilts and quilters but are just as happy to go their own way, break the rules and see what comes next. Fabric companies are constantly bringing us exciting new modern fabric lines and modern quilters are happy to mix these with solids, with antique sheets, with old feed sack fabrics or with any other fabrics they have on hand. They might be making a very traditional quilt with the fabrics they have chosen, but the fabrics give it a modern feel.

But when you look back through the history of quilting, that is what quilters have always done — they have always played around with traditional designs, come up with new ones and mixed up any variety of the fabrics they have available to them. So what we might think of as modern quilts are just quilts made by today's quilters following those age-old traditions.

If I had to define my quilting style, it might best be described as modern traditional. I am drawn to traditional block designs and traditional quilt layouts and patterns, but I love to make them from fresh, modern fabrics, solids or shot cottons or a mix of all three. Many of the fabrics I think of as fresh and modern are in reality re-workings or new interpretations of traditional quilting fabrics and designs. My quilt, King's Treasure, sticks to the traditional form of a simple pattern made from traditional blocks and uses a fabric line which has a strong traditional feel, so my definition of modern quilting is really just what I am inspired to design and make today, no more than that. ☆

FINISH

———◇———

Quilt Top Center

Using 4 short sashing strips and 3 blocks, sew together in a row starting with the sashing strip and alternating with a block (Section A). Press to the sashing strip. Repeat to make 3 rows.

Lay out the 4 long sashing strips alternating with the 3 block rows. Join a strip to a row, with the strip on top (Section B). Press to the strip. Repeat with all rows and strips, ending with a strip on the bottom.

Borders

Measure the quilt top across the center from top to bottom. Piece the cream border strips to this length and sew to each side of the quilt center (Section C). Press to the borders.

Repeat by measuring across the top from side to side. Piece the cream border strips to this length and sew to the top and bottom (Section D). Press to the borders.

Backing

Piece the backing fabric into a 66" × 66" square.

Quilting

King's Treasure was quilted on a domestic machine using straight lines, 2" apart across the entire top. To make the quilting lines straight, mark them first using a quilting ruler and a hera marker.

Binding

Make 260" of dark print binding and bind.

☆ ☆ ☆

Scenic Road
to the Whitehouse

⇢ Designed and made by Lauren Hunt

⇢ 72" × 72"

Many Roads to the Whitehouse block
Aug. 17, 1955

I chose this block because I thought it had a strong graphic appeal that would easily lend itself to a more contemporary interpretation. I knew I wanted to add complexity to the block, using various tones of the two main colors to add depth and variety, but I initially struggled with how to keep the block construction as simple and efficient as possible. By pairing strip-pieced sets and sewing them together before cutting apart the individual units, I was able to avoid sewing on a bias-cut edge, as well as giving blocks the appearance of far more complex piecing than is actually done. ☆

⇢ Lauren

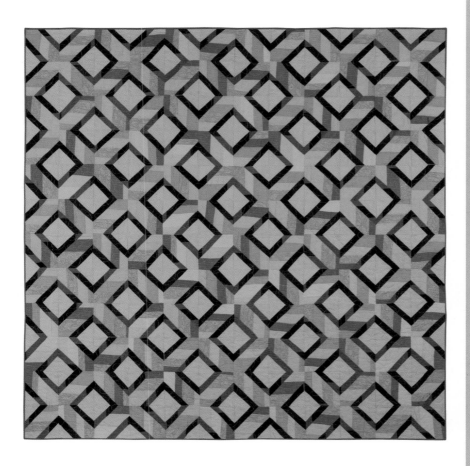

GATHER

4 ¾ yards total of a variety of blue and indigo prints and solids for blocks

4 ¾ yards total of a variety of gold and green prints and solids for blocks

2 ¾ yards of light tan solid for blocks

4 ½ yards of dark blue solid for backing

⅝ yard of blue solid for binding

CUT

Blocks

Blue/indigo and gold/green block fabrics in a variety of widths from 1 ½" to 4" × the width of fabric. Cut a minimum of 72 strips of each colorway. Stack according to color.

144 — 5" × 5" light tan squares. Cut each in half to make 288 triangles for block corners.

Binding

8 — 2 ½" × the width of fabric blue solid strips.

SEW

144 blocks

6" × 6" (finished)

Randomly select 2 blue/indigo strips and sew together on the long edge. Press seams to one side. Repeat with the remaining strips to make 36 pairs. Sew 2 pairs together to make 18 panels at least 7" × the width of fabric.

Repeat with the gold/green fabrics to make 18 panels at least 7" × the width of fabric.

Pair the blue/indigo sets with gold/green sets, and place them right sides together, making sure the seams are going in the opposite direction. Pin a few times in the center of the strip sets to stabilize them for the next step.

Starting at the bottom-left edge of the sets, use an acrylic ruler and a marking pen to draw a 45-degree line across the sets, as shown in the diagram. Then, measure 3" parallel from the first line and draw another at the same angle.

Continue to draw lines at 3" intervals the entire length of the paired strip sets, pinning more between the lines, if necessary, to stabilize. You should be able to get 8 — 3" segments from each set. Repeat with the rest of the strip sets.

Starting on the inside edge of the first marked line, sew ¼" from each side of the marked lines, as shown in the diagram. Repeat with the rest of the strip sets.

Use a rotary cutter to cut along all marked lines, between the ¼" seams. Make 8 angled tubes with the wrong sides facing out.

What is modern quilting?

→ Lauren Hunt

I have to admit that I don't really have much of a philosophy when it comes to modern quilting. For the most part, I try to stay out of the definition game when it comes to quilting styles — lots of people far smarter and more philosophically minded than I am have already said more than enough about what "modern" is, as both a style and a movement. It seems to me that since "modern" finds its place in temporal reality, it will inevitably be redefined by every successive generation (unless we get all "post-modern," "post-post-modern" and "meta-modern," which is exhausting), so it seems to me that just sewing whatever we want and letting someone label it later might serve just as well.

I make the quilts that pop into my head, and I don't really spend any time categorizing them as modern or traditional. My inspiration comes from both sides of the tracks, though. Initially I avoided anything having to do with traditional quilting, but when I began working at a quilt shop, the huge variety of work I was exposed to gave me an appreciation for a much wider range of styles. I've learned a lot from the quilters I met through there, and they come from all across the board, style-wise — I think there's inspiration to be found in every nook and cranny of the quilting world. ☆

Next, mark a line down the center of the blue side of the tubes, parallel to the seams on either side. Use scissors to carefully cut the blue/indigo section in half along the line, dividing it in half so it opens up on either side of the gold/green section. Press open as shown in the diagram. Repeat with all the pieced tubes.

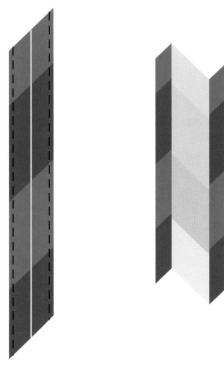

Sew the light tan triangles to either side of the blue strips and press to the triangles. Trim to 6½" × 6½" square as shown in the diagram.

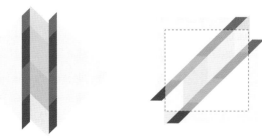

Repeat with the remaining panels to make a total of 144 blocks.

Sew 4 blocks together as a four-patch unit to create 36 blocks. Press seams open.

FINISH

Quilt Top

Arrange the blocks in 6 rows of 6 blocks each. Sew together in rows and join the rows, pressing the seams open.

Backing

Piece the backing fabric into a 76" × 76" square.

Quilting

Scenic Road to the Whitehouse was quilted with gold thread in an allover pattern of fat loops.

Binding

Make 320" of blue solid binding and bind.

* ☆ *

Happy Camper

»→ Designed and pieced by Heather Kojan

»→ Quilted by Maria O'Haver

»→ Size 60" × 72"

A Striped Plain Quilt block

Jan. 12, 1944

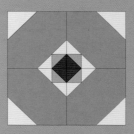

I'm really drawn to quilts with oversized blocks paired with supporting smaller blocks. The bold colors and whimsical patterns of the fabric fit my modern aesthetic. Keep in mind, if you use directional fabrics, you'll have to accommodate for this when cutting the rectangles and corner squares so the fabrics will all line up in the same direction. ☆

Heather

GATHER

⎯◇⎯

⅝ yard each of 4 prints for the large blocks

18 fat quarters of prints for the small and large blocks

1½ yards of cream solid for the small and large block backgrounds

4 yards for backing

⅝ yard of stripe for binding

CUT

⎯◇⎯

Small Blocks

For each block, use cream and 2 coordinating fabrics from the fat quarters and cut the following. Stack the cut units in 14 piles, 1 for each block.

1 — 4¾" × 4¾" print square (a) for the square-in-a-square unit

2 — 3⅞" × 3⅞" cream squares (b). Cut each in half on the diagonal to make 4 triangles for the square-in-a-square unit.

4 — 3½" × 6½" print rectangles (c)

2 — 3⅞" × 3⅞" print squares (d) for half-square triangle units

2 — 3⅞" × 3⅞" cream squares (d) for half-square triangle units

Large Blocks

For each block, use cream and 3 coordinating prints from the remaining fat quarters and 1 — ⅝-yard cut and cut the following. Stack the cut units in 4 piles, 1 for each block.

From the fat quarters

1 — 4¾" × 4¾" print square (A) for the square-in-a-square unit

2 — 3⅞" × 3⅞" print squares (B). Cut each in half on the diagonal to make 4 small triangles.

2 — 4⅞" × 4⅞" print squares (C). Cut each in half on the diagonal to make 4 medium triangles.

From ⅝-yard

2 — 6⅞" × 6⅞" squares (F) for the half-square triangle units

4 — 6½" × 12½" rectangles (E)

From the cream solid

2 — 6⅞" × 6⅞" cream squares (D). Cut each in half on the diagonal to make 4 large triangles.

2 — 6⅞" × 6⅞" cream squares (F) for the half-square triangle units

SEW

Small Blocks

12" × 12" (finished)
Make 14

Each small block is made of 4 half-square triangle units, 1 square-in-a-square unit and 4 rectangles.

Half-Square Triangle Units

Using the print (d) and cream squares (d), make 4 half-square triangle units using the directions in Sewing Basics, page 76. Trim to 3½" × 3½".

Square-in-a-Square Unit

Starting with the center square (a), add 4 small cream triangles (b) to each side using the directions in Sewing Basics, page 76. Trim to 6½" × 6½".

Block Assembly

Make 2

Sew 2 half-square triangle units to either side of 1 rectangle (c). Press to the rectangles.

Sew the remaining 2 rectangles to either side of the square-in-a-square unit. Press to the rectangles.

Join the 3 rows as shown in the diagram to finish.

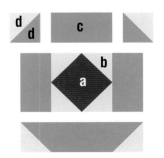

Large Blocks

24" × 24" (finished)
Make 4

The large blocks are made the same as the small blocks with the addition of an extra 2 rounds of triangles in the center square-in-a-square unit.

Half-Square Triangle Units

Using the print squares (F) and cream squares (F), make 4 half-square triangle units using the directions in Sewing Basics, page 76. Trim to 6½" × 6½".

Square-in-a-Square Unit

Using the print center square (A) and 4 print triangles (B), sew 1 square-in-a-square unit using the directions in Sewing Basics, page 76. Trim to 6½" × 6½".

To this unit, add the medium triangles (C) as above. Trim to 9½" × 9½". To finish the center unit, sew the large, cream triangles (D) to all 4 sides. Trim to 12½" × 12½".

Block Assembly

Make 2

Sew 2 half-square triangle units to either side of 1 rectangle (E). Press to the rectangles.

Sew the remaining 2 rectangles to either side of the center unit. Press to the rectangles.

Join the 3 rows as shown in the diagram to finish.

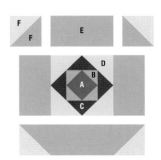

What is modern quilting?

→ Heather Kojan

Modern Quilting is tough to describe. As for design, it's an "I know it when I see it" attitude. I like quilts to look bright and clean. I also want them to be easy and fast. I like blocks rooted in tradition, but given a contemporary spin. (This can mean wonky, supersized, blocks stretched to a rectangle, or a combination. A wonky Dresden? Sure, why not?) Some will describe modern quilting as "breaking the rules" or "anything goes." But I believe you have to know the rules first before you can break them. Good design and technique are the foundation of great quilts.

Modern quilting also encompasses the way we interact as quilters. When I first started my quilting journey, I knew three other quilters, and two of them owned the one quilt shop in town. My quilting was solitary. Through social media, I know hundreds of quilters. (Well, I follow hundreds of quilting blogs, and I feel like I know the quilters. It's kind of the same, right?) At any given moment, I can connect with another quilter, get an idea, offer an opinion, search a technique or just sit back and watch the show. And with all of the modern quilt guilds across the world, I know there will always be an IRL friend in every new city I go to. With modern quilting, I feel like I'm part of a vibrant, generous community. ☆

FINISH

Quilt Top

The top is assembled in 4 quadrants and the quadrants are then sewn into 2 halves and the halves are joined to finish the top.

Referring to the assembly diagram, and the photo of the quilt on page 25, determine which blocks you want in each quadrant, paying attention to color and value. Press seams to one side throughout.

Quadrant A

Make 2

Sew 3 small blocks together in a row. Sew the remaining 2 blocks together. Join the 2 blocks to the side of the large block. Finish by sewing the 3-block row to the top.

Quadrant B

Make 2

Sew 2 small blocks together and join to the bottom of the large block.

Sew each Quadrant A and Quadrant B together, as shown in the diagram. Join the two halves together to finish.

Backing

Piece the backing fabric into a 66" × 78" square.

Quilting

Happy Camper is quilted with an all over "woodsy" theme of oak leaves and acorns to match the fabrics.

Binding

Make 285" of stripe binding and bind.

✻ ☆ ✻

Pinwheels

» Designed and made by John Kubiniec

» Size 69" × 84"

Spider Web block
Jan. 23, 1929

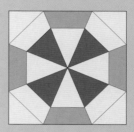

The traditional Spider Web block has only two divisions in each wedge and is normally made up of colors that are not part of the background or negative space. I decided to add the background fabric/negative space color to the block so that the negative space would be incorporated into the actual block design. Also by placing the background fabric on the edge of the wedges and including sashing that is the same color as the background/negative space fabric, the negative space is drawn into the design and alters the actual block design, giving the block the appearance of floating. ☆

» John

GATHER

⅔ yard of red solid

⅔ yard of green solid

⅓ yard of pink solid

⅓ yard of purple solid

¾ yard of yellow solid

½ yard of blue solid

6 yards of white for blocks, background and binding

5⅓ yards of light print or solid for backing

Template plastic (for triangle template)

Note: A specialty ruler that makes isosceles triangles for kaleidoscope blocks can be used to make wedges rather than making the template. The Kaleido-Ruler from Marti Michell was used to make this quilt. Ask at your local quilt shop for others.

CUT

Blocks

Red
4 — 2½" × width of fabric strips
2 — 5½" × width of fabric strips

Green
2 — 5½" × width of fabric strips
4 — 2½" × width of fabric strips

Pink
3 — 2" × width of fabric strips

Purple
3 — 2" × width of fabric strips

Yellow
12 — 2" × width of fabric strips

Blue
8 — 2" × width of fabric strips

White
18 — 2" × width of fabric strips
4 — 5½" × width of fabric strips
8 — 2½" × width of fabric strips
5 — 4⅜" × width of fabric strips
    for the corner triangles. Subcut
    into 40 — 4⅜" × 4⅜" squares.
    Cut each square in half on the
    diagonal to make 80 triangles.

Sashing

11 — 3½" × width of fabric strips. Subcut into 15 — 12½" strips. Piece the remaining strips together and cut into 4 — 57½" strips.

Borders

8 — 6½" × width of fabric strips

Binding

9 — 2½" × width of fabric strips

SEW

20 Blocks

12" × 12" (finished)
Pinwheels are made of 2 different block styles in 5 colorways.

Block Style 1 —
Green and White Outer Ring

Make 4

To make this block, you'll need:
4 — 2½" wide green strips
2 — 5½" wide white strips
4 — 2½" wide white strips
2 — 5½" wide red strips
16 — white triangles

Strip Sets

Sew a green strip to either side of 2 — 5½" white strips to make 2 strip sets. Press to the dark.

Sew a 2½" white strip to either side of 2 red strips to make 2 strip sets. Press to the dark.

Using the template plastic, make the wedge template on page 37 or use a specialty ruler to cut 32 wedges — 16 red and white and 16 white and green. Refer to diagrams for instructions on cutting the wedges.

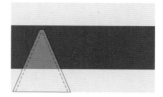

Block Assembly

Sew a corner triangle to each of the 16 green sections. Press to the white triangle.

Sew 1 Red/White section to Green/White section. Press seams to one side. Repeat with remaining wedges. Make 16 pairs.

Sew the pairs together, press seams the same direction as the pairs. Make 8.

Sew 2 sections together to make a half block. Press to the red wedge. Repeat with remaining pairs. Make 8 half blocks.

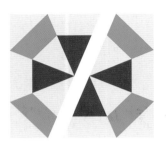

Sew two halves together to form block. Repeat with remaining sections. Make 4 blocks.

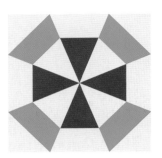

What is modern quilting?

⇨ John Kubiniec

Modern quilting to me is characterized by a rediscovery of negative space in quilts. Space that lets the boldness of a block stand out, or lets the fabric shine. This use of negative space is something that is really very traditional in the world of quilting. One only needs to look at the red and white quilts of the 1800s or the quilts from the 1930s, where the feed sacks were used in conjunction with solids. I think this resurgence in the use of negative space is part of the natural ebb and flow of design. Quilt designs and fabric designs in recent years celebrated color and big, bold designs, and in letting the pattern from one fabric merge into that of another when the patches touched. The time was right for a cleaner, leaner look.

Another aspect of the modern quilt movement is the role of the Internet and social media. Much learning occurs online either through taking online classes, watching homemade videos about techniques and tricks, exploring the world of the blog, Twitter, Pinterest — the list goes on and on. The Internet has thus allowed for a virtual quilting bee to occur. Instead of gathering in someone's home, or the local church or meeting hall, quilters can gather online to meet one another and share, making this a truly global adventure. This sharing has a great deal of freedom — people are allowed to explore different ways of creating quilts, figuring things out on their own, becoming a quilter where "the quilt police" rarely roam, thus allowing a great deal of thinking outside of the box.

All of this, I think, has been a great shot in the arm for the quilting community in general. There are new approaches to quilt designs, new fabric designers that have been brought into the world of quilting, traditional blocks are being rediscovered and given a new look — in short, there is a new freedom in approaching quilt design and construction. My hope is that the flexibility and spontaneity that presently exists in the modern quilt movement continues to live and evolve. ☆

Block Style 1 — Red and White Outer Ring
Make 4

To make this block, you'll need:
4 — 2 ½" wide red strips
2 — 5 ½" wide white strips
4 — 2 ½" wide white strips
2 — 5 ½" wide green strips
16 — white triangles

Strip Sets

Sew a red strip to either side of 2 — 5 ½" white strips to make 2 strip sets. Press to the dark.

Sew a 2 ½" white strip to either side of 2 green strips to make 2 strip sets. Press to the dark.

Cut 32 wedges — 16 green and white and 16 white and red. Finish the block using the same method used for the other Block Style 1. Make 4.

Block Style 2 — Purple and Pink
Make 4

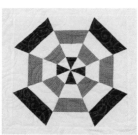

To make this block, you'll need:
3 — 2" wide pink strips
3 — 2" wide purple strips
6 — 2" wide white strips
16 — white triangles

Strip Sets

Sew 3 strip sets of purple/white/pink/white. Press to the dark.

Referring to the diagrams, cut 32 wedges — 16 with a white point and 16 with a purple point.

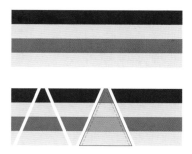

Assembly

Sew the white triangles to the wedges that have a purple strip on the bottom. Press to the triangle. Finish the block using the same method used for Block 1. Make 4.

Block Style 2 — Yellow and Blue Outer Ring
Make 5

To make this block you'll need:
8 — 2" wide yellow strips
4 — 2" wide blue strips
4 — 2" wide white strips
20 — white triangles

Strip Sets

Sew 4 strip sets of yellow/white/yellow/blue. Press to the yellow.

Referring to the photos, cut 40 wedges — 20 with a blue point and 20 with a yellow point.

Assembly

Sew the white triangles to the wedges that have a yellow strip on the bottom. Press to the triangle. Finish the block using the same method used for the other Block Style 2. Make 5.

Block Style 2 —
Yellow and White Outer Ring
Make 3

To make this block, you'll need:
4 — 2" wide yellow strips
4 — 2" wide blue strips
8 — 2" wide white strips
12 — white triangles

Strip Sets

Sew 4 strip sets of yellow/white/blue/white. Press to the white.

Cut 24 wedges — 12 with a yellow point and 12 with a white point.

Assembly

Sew the white triangles to the wedges that have a yellow strip on the bottom. Press to the triangle. Finish the block using the same method used for the other Block Style 2. Make 3.

FINISH

Quilt Top Center

Determine placement of the blocks by arranging them in 5 rows of 4 blocks each on your design wall or floor. Once you have decided, insert 3 sashing strips in between each block in each row. Sew the rows together (Section A). Press to the sashing. Repeat to make 4 rows.

To finish the top center, alternate the block rows and the long sashing strips (Section B), starting with a block row, and sew the quilt top center together. Press to the sashing strips.

Borders

Measure the quilt top across the center from top to bottom. Piece the white border strips to this length and sew to each side of the top center (Section C). Press to the borders.

Repeat by measuring across the top from side to side. Piece the white border strips to this length and sew to the top and bottom of the top center (Section D). Press to the borders.

Backing

Piece the backing fabric to make the backing 75" × 90".

Quilting

Pinwheels was quilted with a simple swirl and circle design to give a sense of the wind blowing across the quilt to make the "pinwheels" spin.

Binding

Make 326" of white binding and bind.

☆ ☆ ☆

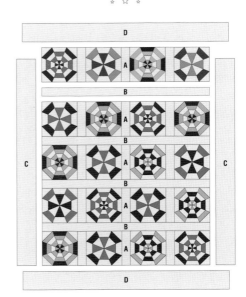

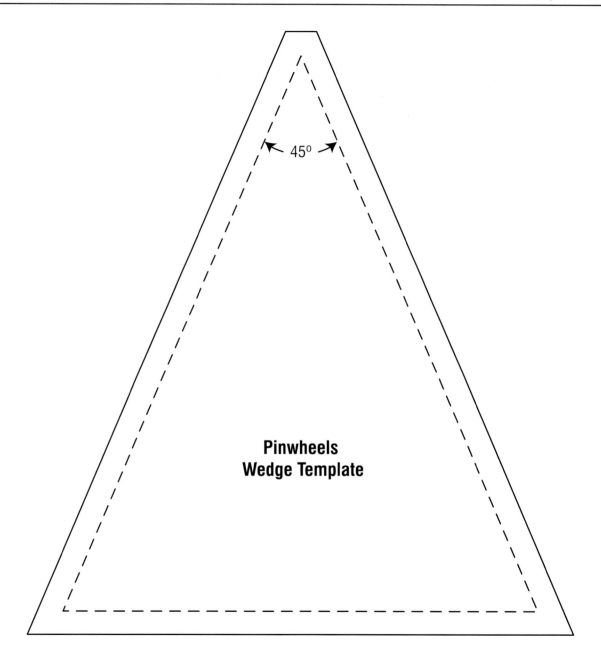

45°

**Pinwheels
Wedge Template**

Trace the wedge template onto the template
plastic and cut out on the line. The same template
is used to cut all the wedges. Align the bottom
edge of the template with the edge of the panel.

Blaze

→ **Designed and made by Adrianne Ove**

→ **Size 60" × 84"**

Based on
The Star of Bethlehem block
April 28, 1937

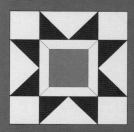

To start the creative process, I like to write down words to guide the artistic theme of a quilt. For *Blaze*, I chose graphic, colorful and playful. The black and white centers were chosen to be graphic and repetitive, adding weight to the stars and bringing part of the background colors all the way through the quilt. By keeping all of the centers the same, it brings the focus back to the star points. The varied angles of the star points add even more interest and movement. The repetitive block setting makes the small nuances of each star shine and adds a vintage feel. ☆

→ Adrianne

GATHER

⸺◇⸺

⅔ yard white solid

⅓ yard of black textured print

1 fat quarter each of red, orange, yellow, chartreuse, dark blue-green, light blue-green, dark purple, light purple and medium gray

18 fat quarters of light prints for block background

5 yards of light print for backing

⅝ yard of light blue for binding

CUT

⸺◇⸺

Blocks

35 — 2½" × 2½" squares of black for block center

70 — 1½" × 2½" strips of white solid for block center

70 — 1½" × 4½" strips of white solid for block center

140 — 4½" × 4½" squares of the solid fat quarters for star points. Cut each square in half on the diagonal to make 280 triangles.

280 — 4½" × 4½" squares of light prints for background

Binding

8 — 2½" strips × width of fabric strips of light blue

SEW

—◄◊►—

35 Blocks

12" × 12" (finished)

Block Center Units

Make 35

Sew 2 short white strips to the sides of 1 black square. Press to the dark.

Sew 2 long white strips to the sides of 1 black square. Press to the dark.

Star Point Units

Make 140

For each unit, choose 1 background square and 2 different solid triangles.

Referring to the diagram, sew 1 triangle to the bottom right corner of the square at an angle. Do not mark — the slight variations will make your stars sparkle! Cut away the background triangle, leaving ¼" seam allowance, and press.

Repeat on the bottom left corner with the second colored triangle.

Trim the unit to 4 ½" × 4 ½". Repeat to make 140 units.

Block Assembly

For each block you will need 1 center unit, 4 star point units and 4 assorted background squares.

Lay out the units as shown in the diagram and sew together into rows. Press seams open. Sew the rows together and press.

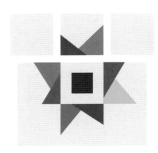

»→ Adrianne Ove

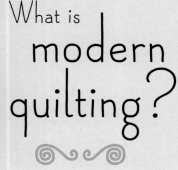

What is modern quilting?

Here are some of my favorite elements that are found in modern design and modern quilting:

- Clean lines
- Graphic patterns
- Pure, bold colors mixed with neutrals
- Use of basic shapes in new ways
- Functional lines and curves
- Use of color for impact
- Minimalism
- Improvisation

Modern design has been around for a long time, and quilting has been around even longer, but bringing the two together is a relatively new concept. Modern quilters draw upon the experience, tradition and heritage of quilting while transforming the aesthetic to reflect a more streamlined, graphic environment. It is a fun challenge to reinterpret something that has been around for a long time and make it feel new. Simply adding just one or two elements of modern design to a traditional quilt or quilt block can change the entire feel of the original.

In my own work, I think a lot about color, the ratio and placement of color, and the intentional use of neutrals. Neutrals and negative space make the colorful pieces stand out. Instead of a harmonious mix, I like to choose colors that play off each other, adding life and movement to a quilt. Negative space adds weight and importance to the blocks that are included. For a graphic look, I choose contrasting fabrics and simple shapes. Simple, repetitive shapes are so versatile. They can be placed in a traditional row layout or not. They can be improvised or not. Small changes can make a big impact. ✫

FINISH

Quilt Top

Lay out the blocks in 7 rows of 5 blocks each. Sew into rows and join the rows. Press seams open.

Backing

Piece the backing fabric into a 66" × 90" square.

Quilting

Blaze was quilted on a domestic machine in straight lines, ¼" from the seams.

Binding

Make 308" of light blue binding and bind.

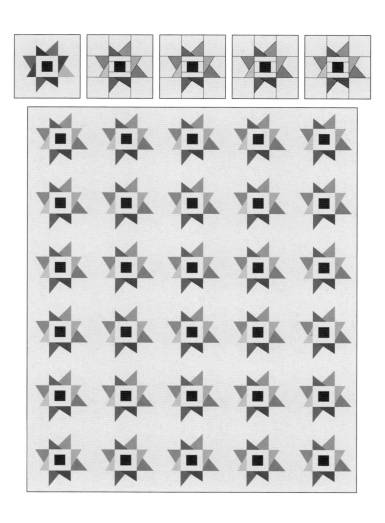

Leave a Light On

⇒ Designed and made by Trisch Price

⇒ 78" × 84"

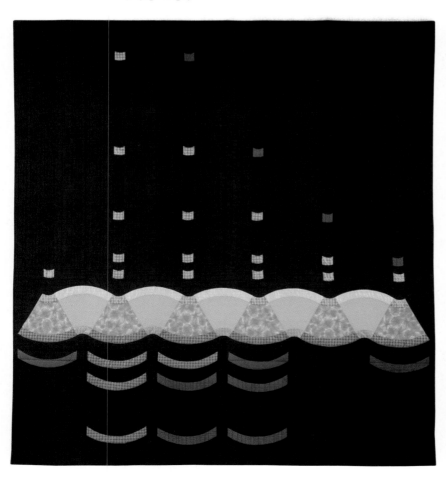

Based on

Air-Ship Propeller block

July 12, 1933

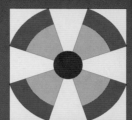

To design this quilt, I played with the block design for quite some time. I tried layouts using differing size block, changing the proportion of the blocks, and off-setting the pieces of the block. In the end, I broke the block into the obvious quadrants. I wanted to put the quadrants next to each other and rotate them back and forth. I changed the quadrant to use an equilateral triangle as the base of the block. After designing the line of blocks, I did want to expand the blocks beyond the line of block. I broke the blocks into its component pieces and echoed them in the negative spaces. ☆

⇒ Trisch

GATHER

——◇——

½ yard bright aqua print for blocks

¼ yard light aqua print for blocks

¼ yard cream print for blocks

½ yard light gray print for blocks and accents

½ yard bright green print for blocks

½ yard light green solid for blocks

¼ yard medium gray solid for accents

7 ½ yards of dark gray solid for blocks, accents, background and binding

5 yards black solid for backing

Template plastic

Small rotary cutter for cutting small curves (optional)

CUT

——◇——

Blocks

Using the templates on pages 50–53, make 11 templates from the template plastic and cut the following;

From bright aqua, cut 6 from Template D and cut 4 from Template G

From light aqua, cut 5 from Template B

From light gray, cut 6 from Template B and 16 from Template J

From cream, cut 5 from Template D

From bright green, cut 6 from Template C

From light green, cut 5 from Template C

From medium gray, cut 7 from Template G and 4 from Template J

From dark gray, cut 11 from Templates A, E, F and H and cut 20 from Templates I–K.

Background

See the diagrams on page 49 for cutting the dark gray background fabrics for Section A and Section C.

For the ends of the pieced blocks in Section B (Q), page 48, cut 1 — 7 ⅝" × 13 ½" strip. Cut in half diagonally to make 2 wedges with a 60-degree angle.

Note: If you are using a print for the background, cut 2 rectangles. Place them right sides together and cut on the diagonal. Use 2 for the ends of the section and reserve the other 2 for another project.

Binding

9 — 2 ½" × width of fabric strips

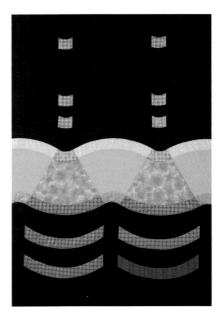

SEW

Blocks

11 Blocks

The blocks are curve pieced in a triangular configuration.

Referring to the diagrams, lay out the 5 pieces (templates A–E) for each block. Sew together and press to one side. Make 6 bright blocks and 5 light blocks.

Large Pieced Accent Units

11 Units
4" × 11" (finished)

Referring to the diagram, lay out 2 dark gray pieces and 1 center piece (templates F–H). Sew together and press to one side. Make 4 bright aqua units and 7 gray units.

Small Pieced Accent Units

20 Units
2" × 3" (finished)

Referring to the diagram, lay out 2 dark gray pieces and 1 center piece (templates I–K). Sew together and press to one side. Make 4 medium gray units and 16 light gray units.

What is **modern** quilting?

» Trisch Price

I think of modern quilting in the same way that I think of **modern design,** modern art and modern architecture. They are all based on traditional techniques and materials, but with a new, unique aesthetic. Modern quilting has a simple essence about it. The lines are simple whether they are straight or organic — though the construction may be complicated. Nothing about the quilt is particularly fussy. The design is mindful of the quilt in its entirety. The colors are usually pure and saturated often engaging high value contrast. Even the fabrics used in modern quilts are typically simple in design, without a lot of shading or fussiness in the design.

FINISH

—◆—

Quilt Top

The top is assembled in 3 sections and the sections are then sewn together to finish the top. The diagrams on page 49 show the sizes to cut each background strip and how to assemble each section. Once cut and laid out, sew each section together as shown in the diagrams. Press seams to one side.

Section A

Section A is made of 6 pieced strips that are inserted in between 7 plain dark gray background strips. Take care to make sure the accent units are all going in the same direction. Press all seams to the long strips.

Section B

Sew 1 bright triangle block to 1 light triangle as shown in the diagram. Be sure to match up the curved pieces so it makes a continuous curve from block to block. Make 5 pairs with 1 bright block leftover. Join the pairs and sew the bright block to the end so you have a row that starts and ends with a bright block, pointing up. Add the background triangles (Q) to each end.

Section B

Section C

Section C is made of 5 pieced panels that are inserted in between 8 plain dark gray background strips. Refer to the diagram for assembly. Take care to make sure the accent units are all going in the same direction. Press all seams to the background.

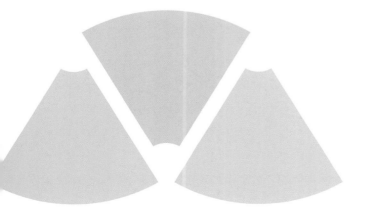

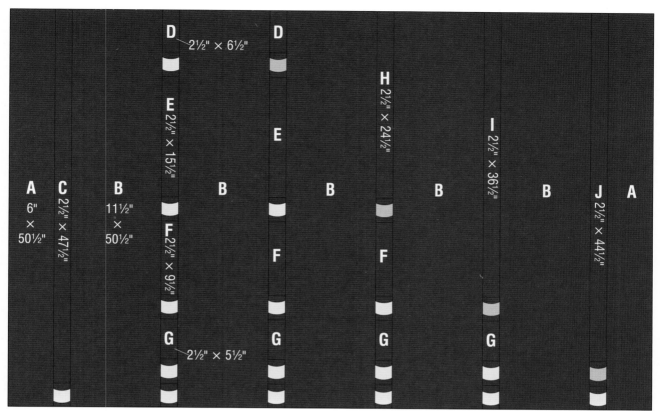

Section A

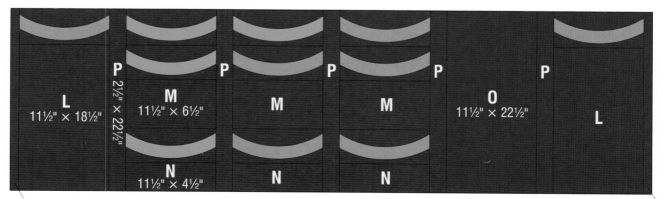

K 1½" × 22½"

Section C

Assembly

Sew the 3 sections together to complete the top.

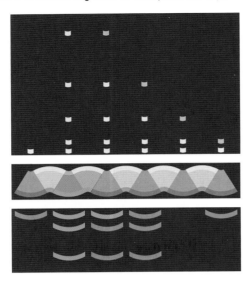

Backing

Piece the backing fabric to 84" × 90".

Quilting

Leave a Light On is quilted in the background with vertical lines. The triangle blocks alternate between swirls in the light green and pebbles in the dark green.

Binding

Make 344" of binding and bind.

☆ ☆ ☆

HOW TO MAKE TEMPLATES C–H

Cut a piece of paper larger than the templates on pages 51-53 and fold it in half, making a deep crease on the folded edge. Unfold and align the crease with the edge of the template marked "place on fold." Trace the template half. Refold on the crease, and cut out on the solid line. Unfold the template and trace the full-size template onto the plastic template.

Leave a Light On Template I

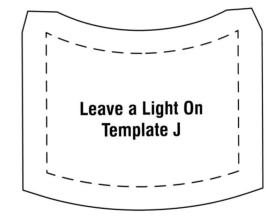

Leave a Light On Template J

Leave a Light On Template K

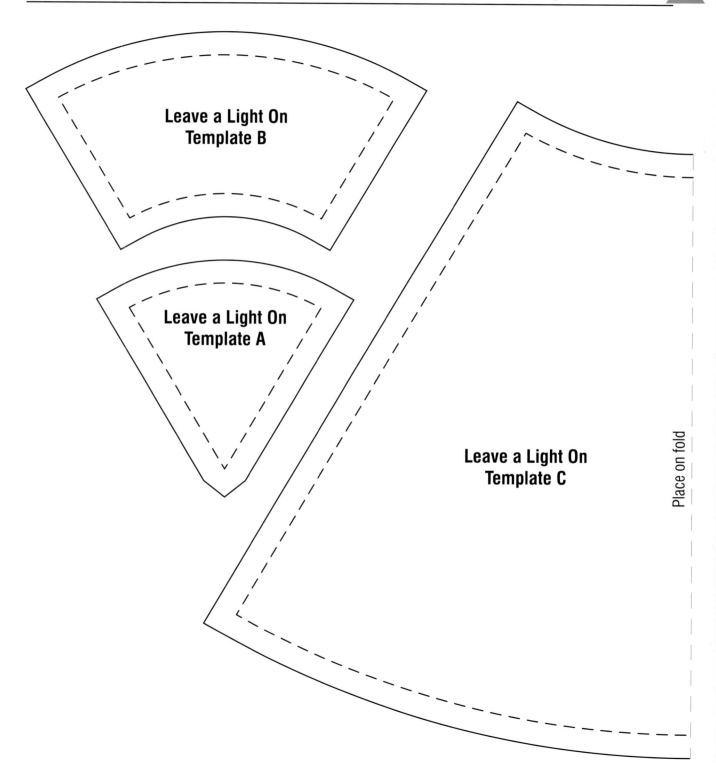

**Leave a Light On
Template B**

**Leave a Light On
Template A**

**Leave a Light On
Template C**

Place on fold

Leave a Light On
Template E

Leave a Light On
Template D

Place on fold

Place on fold

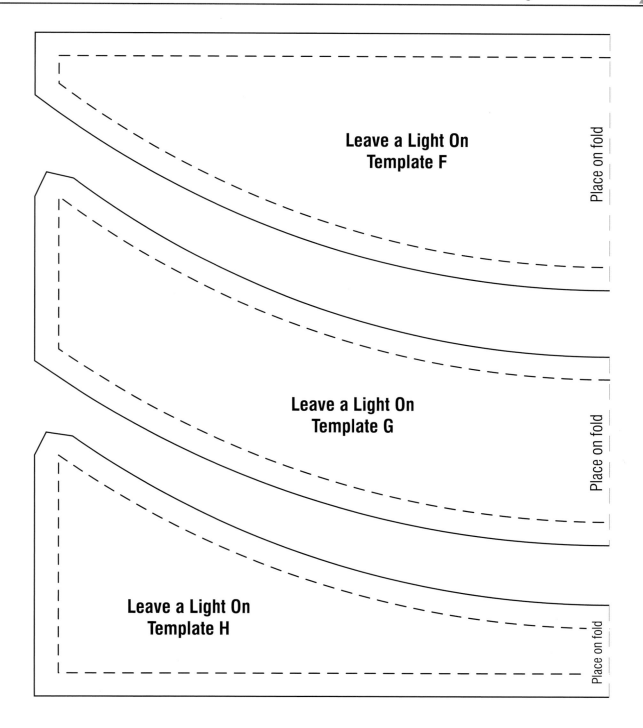

**Leave a Light On
Template F**

Place on fold

**Leave a Light On
Template G**

Place on fold

**Leave a Light On
Template H**

Place on fold

Diamonds in the Rough

» **Designed and pieced by Tammie Schaffer**

» **Quilted by Tia Curtis**

» **59½" × 76"**

Based on
Depression block
May 13, 1937

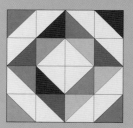

This block is such a simple one and looks fabulous on its own. I am really drawn to quilts that use improv piecing or paneling. So for this quilt, I decided to frame the blocks and float them in a sea of solids. I threw in a couple of prints just for fun! ☆

» Tammie

GATHER

This quilt can be as scrappy or as controlled as you like. For a scrappier look, gather more fabrics in smaller amounts. Be sure to look through your scraps first, then fill in the rest with purchased fabric.

8–10 fat quarters in a variety of pink, orange, yellow and gray prints for the blocks

1 ⅓ yards of cream solid for blocks

5–6 fat quarters in a variety of pink, yellow, mustard and medium gray prints and solids for the background

2 yards of light gray for the background

5 yards of dark gray for the background, backing and binding

CUT

Small Blocks

48 — 2⅜" × 2⅜" print squares
48 — 2⅜" × 2⅜" cream squares

Medium Blocks

32 — 3⅜" × 3⅜" print squares
32 — 3⅜" × 3⅜" cream squares

Large Blocks

16 — 4⅞" × 4⅞" print squares
16 — 4⅞" × 4⅞" cream squares

Background

See the diagrams on pages 58 for exact cutting or improv piece as you go.

Binding

6 — 2½" × width of fabric dark gray strips

2 — 2½" × 14" print strips (can be the same or 2 different prints)

SEW

Small Blocks

6" × 6" (finished)
Make 6

Using the 48 small print squares and 48 small cream squares, make 96 half-square triangle units following the directions in Sewing Basics, page 76. Trim to 2" × 2".

Divide the units into 6 piles of 16 units. Arrange each pile into 4 rows of 4 units each, making sure they are configured as shown in the diagram. Sew each row together and press the seams open. Join the rows to finish.

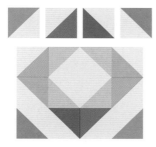

Medium Blocks

10" × 10" (finished)
Make 4

Using the 32 medium print squares and 32 medium cream squares, make 64 half-square triangle units following the directions in Sewing Basics, page 76. Trim to 3" × 3".

Divide the units into 4 piles of 16 units. Arrange each pile into 4 rows of 4 units each, making sure they are configured as shown in the diagram. Sew each row together and press the seams open. Join the rows to finish.

Large Blocks

16" × 16" (finished)
Make 2

Using the 16 large print squares and 16 large cream squares, make 32 half-square triangle units following the directions in Sewing Basics, page 76. Trim to 4½" × 4½".

Divide the units into 2 piles of 16 units. Arrange each pile into 4 rows of 4 units each making sure they are configured as shown in the diagram. Sew each row together and press the seams open. Join the rows to finish.

FINISH

Quilt Top

The top is assembled in 4 quadrants, and the quadrants are then sewn into panels. The panels are joined to finish the top. The following diagrams show the sizes to cut each background strip and square. Refer to the photo of the quilt for color placement or experiment on your own. Once cut and laid out, sew each quadrant together as shown in the diagrams.

If you prefer to take a more improvisational approach, place the blocks on your design wall, moving them around until you get a placement you like. From there, frame each block and fill in the areas around the blocks with different widths and lengths of strips, paying attention to distribute the colors throughout the entire top making sure they are balanced. Think of it as a giant puzzle and have fun!

Tip: Take pictures of your final layout to use as a reference so you don't lose your way when you start sewing.

Quadrant A

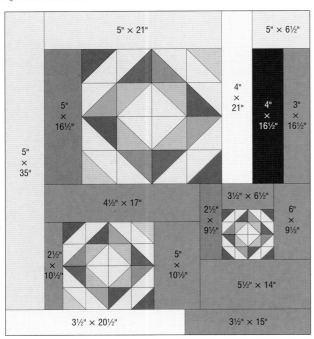

Quadrant C

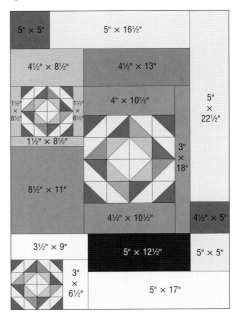

Quadrant B

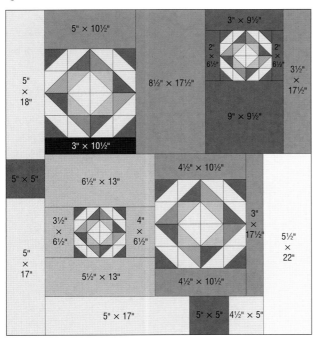

Quadrant D

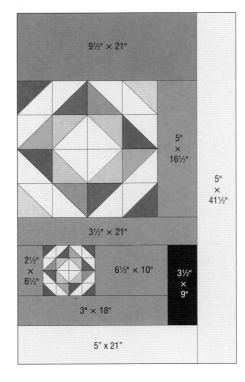

Assembly

Referring to the assembly diagram, sew Quadrant A to Quadrant B. Press. Sew Quadrant C to Quadrant D. Press. Sew the 2 panels together to finish.

Backing

Piece the leftover fabrics from the top, inserting additional dark gray when necessary to make the backing 71" × 88".

Quilting

Straight lines fill the diamonds and the outer border of *Diamonds in the Rough*. The background is filled with swirls to contrast the angles formed by the straight lines.

Binding

Sew the 2 print binding strips to the ends of 2 gray binding strips and join all the strips together, making sure the print strips fall on 2 different edges of the quilt when sewn. Make 290" of binding and bind.

★ ☆ ★

What is modern quilting?

⇒ Tammie Schaffer

For me, modern quilting is more about connecting and sharing online, and the fashion-forward fabrics, rather than the actual style of the quilts. Like many new stitchers, I learned to quilt on the Internet. Back in 2007, I fell in love with blogs and started my own, www.craftytammie.com. I began swapping charm squares on Flickr to build a stash and my love of precuts and fabric swaps continues today! I enjoy seeing traditional blocks stitched up using modern fabrics and color combinations. ☆

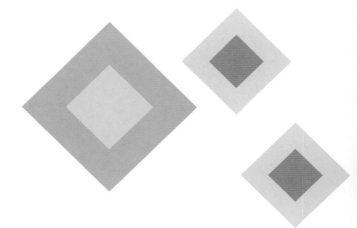

Modern Red Cross

» Designed and pieced by Amy Smart

» Quilted by Melissa Kelley

» 63" × 81"

Based on
Red Cross Quilt block
Oct. 28, 1942

I love traditional quilt blocks, and it's so fun to see their influence on modern quilts. To give this block a modern twist, I blew up the scale of the original block and added more negative space with the solid white to create a secondary design element to the quilt. ✶

» Amy

GATHER

¼ yard cuts of at least 8 red prints and solids for blocks

½ yard of blue solid for blocks

3 ½ yards of white solid for blocks, sashing and borders

¼ yard of red solid for cornerstones

1 ¼ yards each of 4 assorted red prints and solids to total 5 yards for backing

⅝ yard of red gingham for binding

CUT

Blocks

Cut 48 of each of the following:
3 ½" × 3 ½" white solid squares
1 ½" × 3 ½" blue solid strips
1 ½" × 4 ½" blue solid strips
2" × 4 ½" white solid strips
2" × 6" white solid strips
3" × 6" red solid and print strips
3" × 8 ½" red solid and print strips

Sashing

31 — 2 ½" × 16 ½" white solid sashing strips
20 — 2 ½" × 2 ½" red solid cornerstones

Borders

8 — 4" × 42" white solid strips

Binding

8 — 2 ½" × width of fabric red gingham strips

SEW

Blocks

Make 12
16" × 16" (finished)
Each block is made of 4 chevron units.

Chevrons

48 units
8" × 8" (finished)

Sew a short blue strip to the white square. Press to the dark. Add the long blue strip to the adjacent side and press to the dark.

Repeat on the next round with the 2 white strips.

Finish the unit by sewing on the 2 red strips.

The finished chevron unit.

Block Assembly

Choose 4 chevron units with the most variety of red prints and sew together with the red strips to the inside of the block.

modern quilting?

⇢ Amy Smart

If asked to choose, I don't know that I could pick a favorite style of quilting, other than to say "scrappy, with lots of different fabrics." Maybe that's why pioneer quilts and depression-era quilts are some of my favorites — they have a "make it do" sensibility about them, using up whatever leftover bits of fabric were on hand to create a work of art. And for me, the randomness of the colors and prints makes the quilt that much more interesting.

I think this same scrappy, "throw-it-all-in" idea works well with my view on modern quilting as well. Personally, what appeals to me most about the modern quilting movement is the use of negative space or wide areas of typically solid fabric so show off the design of the quilt in general, and the pretty fabrics specifically. That solid is also a great unifier, allowing the use of lots of different colors and prints and tying them all together. I personally tend to use a lot of white fabric for this purpose because I like how clean it looks, but I am trying to break out of that rut and use other colors and even prints for the negative space to show off the design, colors and fabrics.

I also love the modern aspect of taking traditional blocks and motifs and by changing the scale of the block and the style of fabrics (using all solids, for example) can give the design a fresh, modern aesthetic. I will say, I'm not a purist when trying to define modern quilting because I think the term modern implies continuous exploration of design and pushing of boundaries. ☆

Sashing

Lay out 3 blocks and 4 sashing strips. Sew together in a row, starting with a sashing strip (Section A). Press to the sashing strip. Repeat to make 4 rows.

Lay out 3 sashing strips and 4 cornerstone units. Sew together on the short ends, starting with a corner stone (Section B). Press to the sashing. Repeat to make 5 strips.

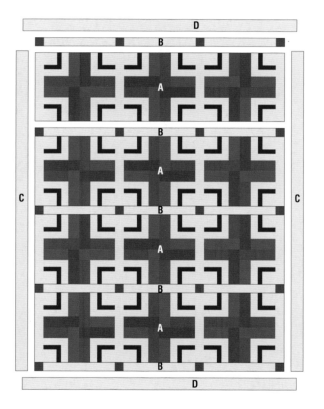

FINISH

Quilt Top Center

Alternate the sashing strips and block rows, starting with a sashing strip and sew the quilt top center together. Press to the sashing strips.

Borders

Measure the quilt top across the center from top to bottom. Piece the white border strips to this length and sew to each side of the top center (Section C). Press to the borders.

Repeat by measuring across the top from side to side. Piece the white border strips to this length and sew to the top and bottom of the top center (Section D). Press to the borders.

Backing

Piece the red solid and prints to make the backing 75" × 93".

Quilting

Modern Red Cross was quilted with an allover square "stipple" pattern, accenting all the angles of the design.

Binding

Make 310" of red gingham binding and bind.

✧ ☆ ✧

Electric Fans

→ Designed and pieced by Susan Strong

→ Quilted by Ardelle Kerr

→ 60" × 82 ½"

Based on
Rebecca's Fan block
May 28, 1938

As soon as I looked at the original Rebecca's Fan block, I knew exactly what I would do to give it a more modern look. I wanted the blocks to float on the background, so I decided to alternate the colored wedges and background wedges in each block. The colored wedges were pieced with a strip of background to add to the illusion of the block floating and to give a circular shape to the fans. The color palette, along with the asymmetrical block setting, helps to turn a traditional block into a modern quilt. ✩

→ Susan

GATHER

4 — ¼ yard cuts each of assorted turquoise, gray, blue and green print for blocks

6 ½ yards of light gray solid for blocks, background and binding

5 yards of gray print for backing

Paper piecing papers

Template plastic (for wedge template)

CUT

Blocks

12 — 7" × the width of fabric strips from the 4 turquoise, gray and blue prints

4 — 7 ½" × the width of fabric strips from the 4 green prints

12 circles for appliqué center from the leftover prints

12 — 2" × the width of fabric light gray background strips

4 — 4" x the width of fabric light gray background strips

2 — 11" × the width of fabric light gray background strips

5 — 9" × the width of fabric light gray background strips

Background

53 — 8" × 8" gray squares

Binding

8 — 2 ½" × the width of fabric gray strips

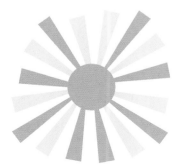

What is modern quilting?

⟫⇢ Susan Strong

I have loved quilting for more than 20 years. I usually have a pretty short attention span when it comes to most activities. But quilting has kept my interest. In fact, my interest has grown. How did that happen? I think it is because quilting is always changing. There are new tools, new techniques, easier or better ways to do old techniques. The fabrics are amazing, in both design and quality. Just when you think that the industry can't come up with anything better, they do. And they do it year after year.

Now there is modern quilting. My definition of modern quilting includes all the commonly expressed elements — asymmetry, negative space, clear colors, improvisational piecing, minimalism, traditional blocks with a new twist, simple graphic design, the use of solid fabrics, etc. Quilts exhibiting any or all of these elements may be considered modern. But I would add another element to my definition

— fun! I love the freedom to take a traditional block or pattern and do something unexpected with it just to see how it turns out.

But more than any of the above elements is the feeling I get when I look at a modern quilt. Modern quilting just makes me happy. And because it makes me happy, I will continue on my modern quilting journey to see where it takes me.

I am reminded of the party game where the first person whispers something in the next person's ear and says to pass it along. The message is passed from person to person, and by the time it gets to the last person, it has usually changed significantly. I think modern quilting is like that, changing as ideas pass from one quilter to the next, which creates a sense of newness.   ☆

SEW

Blocks

Each block and partial block is made of paper-pieced units with an appliqué center. The paper-pieced units are pre-pieced into strip sets and cut with a template.

Strip Sets

Make 16

Sew the 12 — 2" wide background strips to each 7" wide block print strips. Press to the background.

Sew the 4 — 4" wide background strips to each 7 ½" wide green strips. Press to the background.

Template and Cut Wedges

Enlarge 125%, and trace the wedge template, found on page 74, onto the template plastic and cut out on the line. The same template is used to cut all the wedge shapes. Align the narrow end of the template with the edge of the print fabric. The wide end of the template may extend over the edge because of the different lengths of wedges required.

Cut 35 wedges from each color group. Label each stack according to its piecing placement: turquoise: A1; gray: A3; green: A5; and blue: A7.

Cut 105 wedges from the 9" background fabric strips. Stack in 3 piles and label them A2, A6 and A8.

Cut 35 wedges from the 11" background strips. Label the stack A4.

Paper Piecing Units

Make 35

Using the paper piecing template on page 75, prepare 35 patterns for paper piecing. The template will need to be enlarged 125%, then copied onto your paper piecing papers.

Start in the middle of each block and piece out toward the edges as shown in the diagrams. Be sure to match each wedge number with the number on the template so they are sewn in the proper place. Once the unit is pieced, trim to 8" × 8".

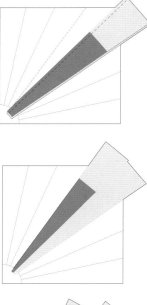

Appliqué Centers

Using the circle template found on page 74 and your favorite appliqué method, prepare 12 center circles for appliqué. Appliqué the circle to the center of the 6 full blocks. For the half-blocks and quarter block, use the whole circle and trim away the excess.

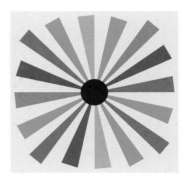

Block Assembly

Make 6 full blocks, 5 half blocks and 1 quarter block

Join 4 paper pieced units and piece together. Press seams to the background fabric. Repeat with 20 more units to make 6 blocks that measure 15½" × 15½".

Sew 2 paper pieced units together. Press seams to the background fabric. Repeat with 8 more units to make 5 blocks that measure 8" × 15½".

You should have 1 unit left over for the quarter block.

Once the blocks are complete, remove the paper from the back side of each block.

FINISH

——◀◊▶——

Quilt Top

The top is sewn together in 9 sections. Each section uses 8" × 8" background squares to fill in around the blocks. Refer to the diagram for piecing each section.

Once the sections are sewn, join them together in 2 columns. Join the columns to finish.

Backing

Piece the backing together to make the backing 66" × 88 ½".

Quilting

Electric Fans is quilted using an alternating combination of straight lines and a free motion design in the background. Each blade is quilted with a ribbon candy design with the center of each fan pebbled.

Binding

Make 305" of light gray binding and bind.

☆ ☆ ☆

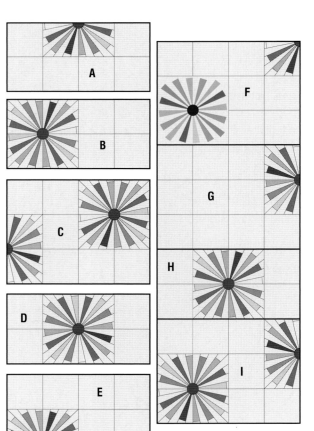

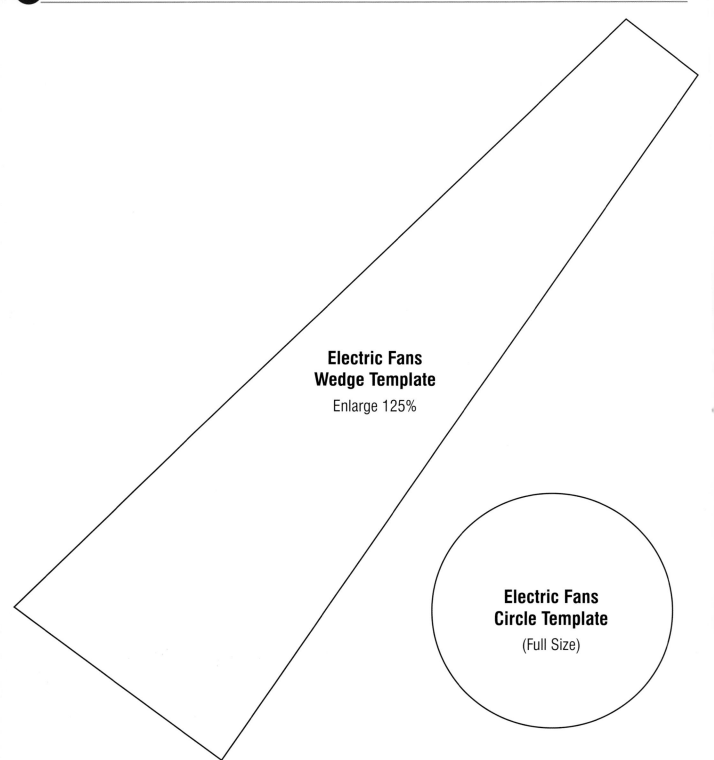

**Electric Fans
Wedge Template**

Enlarge 125%

**Electric Fans
Circle Template**

(Full Size)

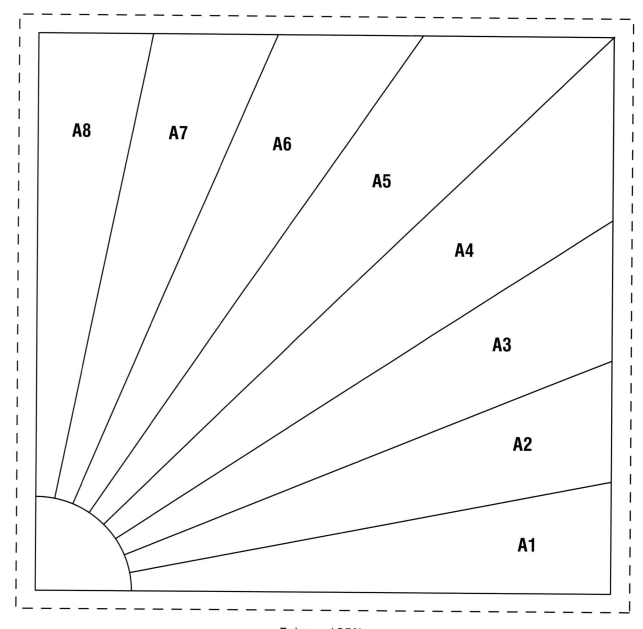

Enlarge 125%

Sewing Basics

The patterns in *Classic Modern Quilts* are written assuming you have a basic level of quiltmaking skills. Paper piecing, curved piecing, simple appliqué and using specialty rulers are part of some of the patterns. Use your favorite methods for these techniques.

The following are the methods used to make half-square triangle units and square-in-a-square units throughout *Classic Modern Quilts*. Each pattern will tell the cutting measurements and finished sizes for each unit.

Half-Square Triangle Units

This method makes 2 half-square triangle units at a time. Each unit is made from 2 squares.

Cut 2 squares ⅞" larger than the finished size of the unit. Draw a line on the back side of the lightest fabric. Match the squares, right sides together. Sew ¼" from either side of the drawn line.

Cut apart on the drawn line.

Press the units open, usually to the dark. Trim to the appropriate size to finish.

Square-in-a-Square Units

Each unit is made of a center square and 4 triangles.

Sew two triangles to either side of the square. Press to the triangles.

Sew the remaining two triangles to the other sides of the square. Press to the triangles. Trim to the appropriate size to finish.

Contributors

LISA CALLE

Lisa's sewing story started with a move to a new town and the purchase of a charming but tiny 1950s ranch house. Wanting to sew some cute things for herself and the new house, she took a series of classes at a local shop. For a couple of years, she sewed garments, bags, and throw pillows. All the while, her fabric stash was multiplying. She realized she could never use it all up making clutches, so she decided to make a quilt. Her first quilt was a Mother's Day gift, and that one quilt turned into an obsession.

In 2010, Lisa founded the Dallas branch of the Modern Quilt Guild and served as president for the first two years. She teaches sewing and quilting and speaks to area quilt guilds about modern quilting.

She's married to a handsome and creative man, and together they have a son. You can follow her adventures and quilting stories at www.vintagemodernquilts.com.

LYNNE GOLDSWORTHY

Lynne is a United Kingdom quilter who loves to combine traditional quilt blocks and designs with modern fabrics. She started quilting about 15 years ago, after a series of business trips to Washington State, where she fell in love with American quilts. It was not easy to find quilting fabrics in the U.K. at the time. Those that she could find did not really appeal to her, so she lost interest quickly. Fast forward 10 years when she met someone in her local village who had just started quilting. She introduced Lynne to modern quilting fabrics and the online quilting community, which was full of inspiration and ideas.

A few months later, Lynne started a blog called Lily's Quilts at www.lilysquilts.blogspot.co.uk. She has had several projects published in U.K. quilting magazines, in quilting books and is co-author of two books that will come out in 2014. Lynne also is part of the team of four that run the online modern quilting magazine, *Fat Quarterly*, at www.fatquarterly.com, and the annual London Fat Quarterly modern quilting retreat.

LAUREN HUNT

When not quilting, Lauren draws and designs fabric that she sells at www.auntjune.etsy.com, and she occasionally rants and rambles in blog-form at www.auntjune.com. She lives in Kansas City, Mo., where she and her husband, Brian, share an ancient house with Baxter-Cat and a schnauzer-mutt, Rufus.

HEATHER KOJAN

Heather has been quilting for more than 20 years, starting with very traditional quilts. About four years ago she discovered modern quilting. It revived her enthusiasm for quilting, so much so that she founded the Baltimore Modern Quilt Guild. She's active in several online swaps and virtual quilting bees and hosts one of her own. She also teaches at a local fiber arts shop in Baltimore. Visit her blog at www.heatherkojan.blogspot.com.

ADRIANNE OVE

Adrianne is a quilter and pattern designer whose fresh, modern quilts are inspired by the sun and sea of her native California coastline. Her designs come to life with her love of color and her ability to take a simple idea and make it modern. She is very active in the online quilting community and served as president of the Bay Area Modern Quilt Guild for two years. She lives in a busy house with her husband and two small children. Visit her blog at www.littlebluebell.com.

JOHN KUBINIEC

John's quilt patterns have appeared in numerous magazines, and he was profiled in the summer 2012 issue of *Les Nouvelles — Patchwork et Création Textile*, the journal of the French Patchwork Association. He taught at The City Quilter in New York and MQX New England Quilt Festival.

John was a runner-up in the 2010 McCall's Quilt Design Star contest and was one of eight finalists in a field of 174. He was a panelist at the American Folk Art Museum's program Quiltmakers: Real Men Quilt in June 2011, and his HQ Story was chosen to be part of Handi Quilter's 2012 Ad Campaign.

John recently moved to Rochester, N.Y., and teaches quilting classes at various locations there and in the Fingers Lakes Region, as well as travels and gives presentations to quilt guilds. Follow him on his blog, www.bigrigquilting.blogspot.com.

TRISCH PRICE

Trisch has been quilting for 20 years. She started with traditional and contemporary quilts and has been making modern quilts for five years. She has been published in *Quilt Arts Gifts* and *Stitch* magazines and has won several local and national awards, including the 2011 Modern Quilt Guild's Project Modern Challenge 3: Organic; the 2010 Machine Quilters Showcase First Place Fashion Shot, Best Use of Color; and in 2012 she was a finalist in McCall's Quilt Design Star contest. Follow her at her blog, www.hadleystreetquilts.com.

TAMMIE SCHAFFER

Tammy is the creative force behind her blog, www.craftytammie.com.

Online, she participates in many bees and swaps. She is a Moda Bakeshop chef and is a quilt block tester for *Quiltmaker's 100 Blocks*. She also is a member of the Kansas City Modern Quilt Guild and the Prairie Patches Quilt Guild in Garnett, Kan. Tammy lives in rural Kansas with her husband and four children, who range in age from 2 to 8. When she's not sewing, you can find her working in the garden and watching her chickens.

AMY SMART

Amy learned to quilt from her mom when she was young, but only started taking it seriously when she had her first baby. Since then, she has worked in a local quilt shop for eight years. She started

designing quilt patterns and teaching beginning quilting classes. In 2008, she started documenting her quilting journey on a blog called Diary of a Quilter at www.diaryofaquilter.com. She lives in Salt Lake City, and when not sewing, she enjoys hiking and going on road trips with her family, watching BBC movies and eating delicious food prepared by other people.

SUSAN STRONG

Susan has been quilting for more than 20 years, and in that time, she has made dozens (and dozens) of quilts, designed several quilt patterns to sell at her local quilt store and taught many quilting classes. In 2004,

she designed a quilt for her son called the Amazing Spider-man Quilt. She entered it in the Creative Stitching & Crafting Alive quilt show in Edmonton, Alberta, Canada, where it won first place for Large Original Design. Recently, she had two quilts — STELLA! and If Kaffe Met Seuss — juried into the QuiltCon 2013 Quilt Show in Austin, Texas.

Susan lives in Wetaskiwin, Alberta, Canada, where she is wife to a very understanding husband, mother of two great adult children and Nana to two beautiful granddaughters, Michelle and Payge. She is an original member of the Wetaskiwin Quilters' Group, which started in 1999. She also belongs to a small but fabulous group of quilters that gets together, whenever schedules allow, to sew, share and inspire. Visit Susan's blog at www.strongstitches.wordpress.com.

☆ ☆ ☆

Acknowledgments

The designers would like to acknowledge the following people and companies who helped them make their quilts.

LISA CALLE

Thanks to Lissa Alexander and all of the wonderful people at Moda Fabrics for providing fabric for *Spring Storms*.

LYNNE GOLDSWORTHY

King's Treasure features Shelburne Falls by Denyse Schmidt for Freespirit Fabrics and Robert Kaufman Essex Linen.

HEATHER KOJAN

Thanks to:

Moda and United Notions for supplying S'More Love by Cosmo Cricket for *Happy Camper*.

All my friends who said, "Really? That's awesome!" when I told them I was going to be in a book.

Tammie Schaffer, who was a great sounding board and cheerleader.

A special thanks to my family, who supported me throughout the process.

JOHN KUBINIEC

Thanks to Laura Jaquinto and Jennifer Varon of Windham Fabrics for providing the fabric, Spin from Windham's basics lines, for *Pinwheels*.

ADRIANNE OVE

Thanks to Gwen Marston for inspiration for the improvised star points (also called liberated or wonky) in *Blaze*.

TRISCH PRICE

Leave a Light On was made with Mirror Ball Dot and Kona Solids.

TAMMIE SCHAFFER

Diamonds in the Rough features 2wenty Thr3e by Cosmo Cricket for Moda and Kona Solids.

✦ ☆ ✦

The photography was taken at Hickory Dickory, located at the West Bottoms Antique Marketplace, Kansas City, Mo.